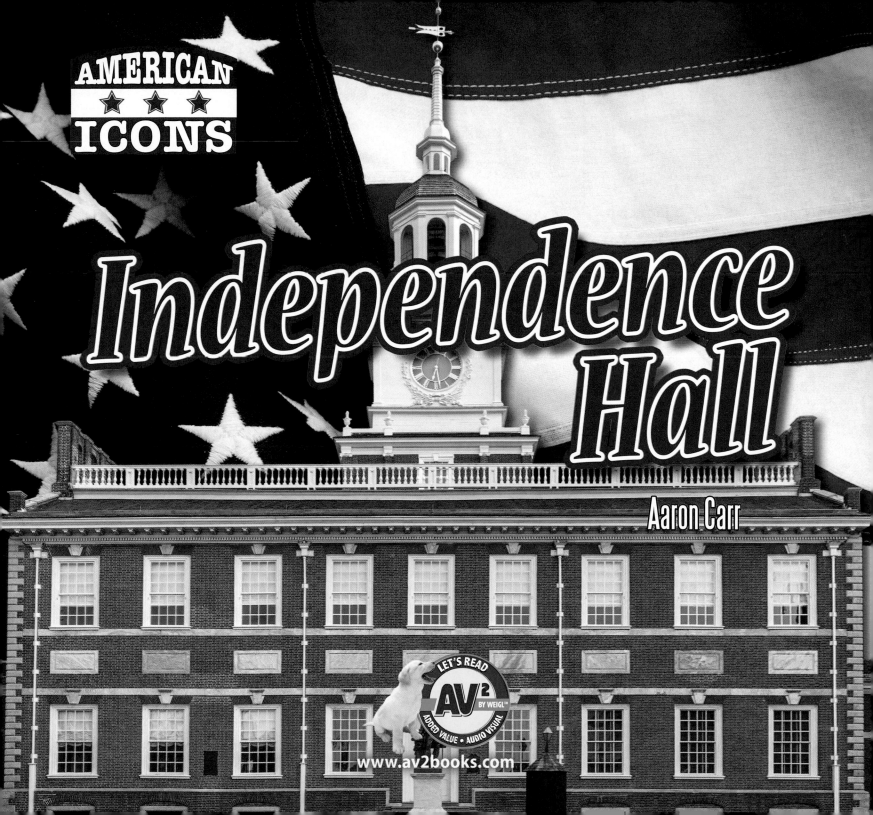

Independence Hall

Aaron Carr

Go to www.av2books.com, and enter this book's unique code.

BOOK CODE

F 1 3 4 6 9 6

AV² by Weigl brings you media enhanced books that support active learning.

AV² provides enriched content that supplements and complements this book. Weigl's AV² books strive to create inspired learning and engage young minds in a total learning experience.

Your AV² Media Enhanced books come alive with...

Audio
Listen to sections of the book read aloud.

Video
Watch informative video clips.

Embedded Weblinks
Gain additional information for research.

Try This!
Complete activities and hands-on experiments.

Key Words
Study vocabulary, and complete a matching word activity.

Quizzes
Test your knowledge.

Slide Show
View images and captions, and prepare a presentation.

... and much, much more!

Published by AV² by Weigl
350 5th Avenue, 59th Floor New York, NY   10118
Websites: www.av2books.com   www.weigl.com

Library of Congress Control Number: 2013953027

ISBN 978-1-4896-0520-7 (hardcover)
ISBN 978-1-4896-0521-4 (softcover)
ISBN 978-1-4896-0522-1 (single-user eBook)
ISBN 978-1-4896-0523-8 (multiuser eBook)

Printed in the United States of America in North Mankato, Minnesota
1 2 3 4 5 6 7 8 9 0 17 16 15 14 13

122013
WEP301113

Every reasonable effort has been made to trace ownership and to obtain permission to reprint copyright material. The publishers would be pleased to have any errors or omissions brought to their attention so that they may be corrected in subsequent printings.

Weigl acknowledges Getty Images as the primary image supplier for this title.

Project Coordinator: Aaron Carr
Designer: Mandy Christiansen

CONTENTS

What Is Independence Hall?

Independence Hall is thought to be the birthplace of America. It is a large brick building in Philadelphia, Pennsylvania.

Article the third
Article the fourth
Article the fifth
Article the sixth
We the People
of the United States
Article I
IN CON
The unanimous Decla
When in the
should declare the causes which impel them to the
with certain unalienable Rights, that among these are
powers from the consent of the governed, — That whe
Government, laying its foundation on such princi
will dictate that Governments long established should not be
evils are sufferable, than to right themselves by abolishing the
evinces a design to reduce them under absolute Despotism, it is their
Bill, according to the Directio
MARYLAND. Dated in ANNA
Anno Domini 1774.
FIVE SH

A National Symbol

Two of the most important events in American history happened at Independence Hall. The Declaration of Independence was signed there. The Constitution was also signed there.

Building the Hall

Workers started to build the hall in 1732. It took 21 years to finish building the hall.

9

Home of the Government

When it was finished, the building was the home of Pennsylvania's government. It was also used for meetings that helped the United States become a country.

The Liberty Bell

The Liberty Bell was put in the tower of Independence Hall. It cracked the first time it was used. The bell was later moved from the tower. It was kept as a symbol of freedom.

The Declaration of Independence

Leaders from the first 13 states agreed to the Declaration of Independence in Independence Hall. They voted to pass this declaration on July 4, 1776. This was the first step in making America free from Great Britain's rule.

The Constitution

In May 1787, leaders from 12 of the first 13 states met in Independence Hall. Together, they wrote the United States Constitution. The Constitution is the highest law of the United States. It lays out the rights and freedoms of all Americans.

Changes

Independence Hall has changed many times over the years. Some parts of the building were taken down. Other parts were made to look different. In 1950, the hall was returned to its 1776 appearance.

Independence Hall Today

Today, Independence Hall is part of Independence National Historical Park. People can visit this park to see Independence Hall, the Liberty Bell, and other important historic places.

21

INDEPENDENCE HALL FACTS

These pages provide detailed information that expands on the interesting facts found in the book. These pages are intended to be used by adults to help young readers round out their knowledge of each national symbol featured in the *American Icons* series.

Pages 4–5

What Is Independence Hall? Independence Hall was the first state house for the Commonwealth of Pennsylvania. It was also one of the most ambitious buildings in the original 13 colonies. For this reason, the state house also served as the base for many important meetings of colonial representatives as they worked to create a new nation. This is why many historians consider Independence Hall the birthplace of the United States.

Pages 6–7

A National Symbol Independence Hall has become an important symbol in the United States because of the role it played in the country's history. The two most important documents in U.S. history are the Declaration of Independence and the Constitution. Both of these documents were drafted and approved in Independence Hall.

Pages 8–9

Building the Hall Construction of the state house began in 1732. The work was funded by the Pennsylvania government, but it could not afford to pay for the whole project at once. Instead, the government paid for the construction in pieces as money became available. This is why the building was not finished until 21 years later, in 1753. Architect Edmund Woolley designed the building with help from lawyer Andrew Hamilton.

Pages 10–11

Home of the Government The state house served as the home of the Pennsylvania state legislature until 1799. This was where all of the laws of Pennsylvania were debated, put to a vote, and passed into law. Before the United States became a country, groups of representatives from each of the colonies gathered in Independence Hall. In this way, the hall acted as the first federal government building.

The Liberty Bell The bell that came to be known at the Liberty Bell started out as an ordinary bell for the Pennsylvania State House bell tower. The bell was rung to announce important government and public meetings. However, the bell cracked the first time it was rung. It was repaired twice, but it eventually cracked again. The Liberty Bell was replaced by the Centennial Bell in 1876.

Declaration of Independence In 1775, representatives from all 13 colonies gathered in Philadelphia for the Second Continental Congress. The Congress met at Independence Hall several times between 1775 and 1783. In that time, they worked out the details of their separation from Great Britain. Though it was not signed until August 2, 1776, the members of the Congress voted on and approved the Declaration of Independence on July 4. This is why the fourth of July is celebrated as Independence Day.

The Constitution In 1786, members of the 13 colonies decided to create a set of laws outlining how the country would be run. Delegates from 12 of the colonies met at Independence Hall in June 1787 for the Constitutional Convention. The Constitution was finished on September 17, 1787, and became law on March 4, 1789. The Constitution outlined the rights of all American people and created the three branches of government.

Changes Independence Hall was made as a Georgian styled red brick building with a tower topped with a wooden steeple. It had three sections, two wings and a central tower. By the 1780s, the steeple had started to rot and was taken down. The wings were demolished from 1811 to 1812. In 1830, the hall was restored in a Greek style. In 1950, the National Park Service restored Independence Hall to its 1776 appearance.

Independence Hall Today Independence Hall is part of Independence National Historical Park in Philadelphia. This park preserves many places and items that played important roles in American history. There are so many historic landmarks in this park that it has been called "America's most historic square mile." The main attractions of the park are Independence Hall, the Liberty Bell Center, and the Benjamin Franklin Museum at Franklin Court.

KEY WORDS

Research has shown that as much as 65 percent of all written material published in English is made up of 300 words. These 300 words cannot be taught using pictures or learned by sounding them out. They must be recognized by sight. This book contains 62 common sight words to help young readers improve their reading fluency and comprehension. This book also teaches young readers several important content words, such as nouns. These words are paired with pictures to aid in learning and improve understanding.

Page	Sight Words First Appearance	Page	Content Words First Appearance
4	a, be, in, is, it, large, of, the, thought, to, what	4	America, birthplace, building, Independence Hall, Philadelphia, Pennsylvania
7	also, American, at, important, most, there, two, was	7	Constitution, Declaration of Independence, events, history, symbol
8	started, took, years	8	workers
11	country, for, home, that, used, when	11	government, meetings, United States
12	as, first, from, later, moved, put, time	12	freedom, Liberty Bell, tower
15	on, states, they, this	15	free, Great Britain, leaders, rule, step
16	all, and, out, rights, together	16	law
19	changes, different, down, has, its, look, made, many, other, over, parts, some, take, were	19	appearance
20	can, people, places, see	20	Independence National Historic Park